RIYA

TRAVEL GUIDE 2024

A Comprehensive Guidebook for Cultural Enthusiasts, Adventure Seekers, and History Buffs – Your Passport to Ancient Marvels, Natural Beauty, and Unforgettable Experiences.

Maryln G. Sloan

Copyright © Maryln G. Sloan, 2024.

All rights reserved. No part of this publication may be reproduced, distributed, or transmitted in any form or by any means, including photocopying, recording, or other electronic or mechanical methods, without the prior written permission of the publisher, except in the case of brief quotations embodied in critical reviews and certain other non-commercial uses permitted by copyright law.

TABLE OF CONTENT

INTRODUCTION
   Welcome to Riyadh!
   About This Guide
   How To Use This Guide
ESSENTIAL INFORMATION
   Location and Geography
   Climate & Weather
   Getting In and Around Riyadh
   Visa requirements
   Currency and Money Matters
   Communication
   Safety Tips
ULTIMATE EXPERIENCES GUIDE IN RIYADH
   Riyadh's top attractions
   Diriyah
MULTIPLE ITINERARIES
   One Day in Riyadh: A Brief Overview
   Two to Three-Day Itinerary
   Family Friendly Itinerary
   Solo Traveler's Guide
HONEST RECOMMENDATIONS FROM LOCALS
   Best Restaurants and Cafes
   Top Hotels and Accommodations

    Vibrant nightlife spots
    Shopping Destinations
    Performing Arts Venues
    Recreational activities.
    Side Trips and Day Excursions

WHAT TO EAT AND DRINK
    Traditional Saudi cuisine
    Popular Local Dishes
    Street Food Delights
    Beverage recommendations

WHAT TO BUY
    Souvenirs and Gifts
    Traditional handicrafts
    Shopping Districts and Markets

TRIP PLANNING TOOLS AND PRACTICAL TIPS
    When to Go: Best Time to Visit Riyadh
    Getting Around The City
    Tips for Beating the Crowd
    Saving Time and Money

HISTORICAL AND CULTURAL INSIGHTS
    Overview of Riyadh's History
    Cultural Etiquettes and Customs
    Architectural Wonders
    Art & Museums
    Cuisine and Culinary Tradition

LOCAL WRITERS' RECOMMENDATIONS
    Locals recommend hidden treasures

Insider tips for exploring Riyadh.
LANGUAGE PRIMER
　　Useful Phrases for Travelers
　　Essential Arabic Phrases for Daily Situations
CONCLUSION
　　Final Thoughts About Visiting Riyadh
　　Your Riyadh adventure awaits!

INTRODUCTION

Welcome to Riyadh!

Welcome to Riyadh, the vibrant capital city of the Kingdom of Saudi Arabia. Riyadh, located in the heart of the Arabian Peninsula, is a bustling metropolis that seamlessly blends modern and traditional elements, offering visitors a unique glimpse into Saudi culture and history. As you begin your tour of this bustling city, prepare to be captivated by its rich history, awe-inspiring architecture, delicious food, and friendly locals.

Riyadh is Saudi Arabia's political, economic, and cultural hub, attracting visitors from all over the world due to its numerous attractions and experiences. Whether you're exploring the towering skyscrapers of the commercial sector, meandering through historic souks brimming with treasures, or immersing yourself in the serene serenity of the desert surroundings, Riyadh provides unforgettable experiences at every turn.

About This Guide

The Riyadh Travel Guide is your comprehensive guide to seeing this magnificent city with ease and confidence. Whether you're a first-time visitor or a seasoned tourist, this book will provide you with all of the essential information, insider insights, and professional recommendations you need to make the most of your time in Riyadh.

Drawing on local knowledge and expertise, this book provides candid insights into the best sights, restaurants, hotels, nightlife, shopping, and more, ensuring that you experience Riyadh like a true insider. From must-see attractions to hidden gems off the main road, we've curated a selection of experiences that capture the essence of Riyadh's unique charm and intrigue.

How To Use This Guide

Navigating a big metropolis like Riyadh can be intimidating, especially for first-time tourists. That's why we designed our guide to be user-friendly and easy to navigate, allowing you to tailor your trip to your specific interests, preferences, and travel style.

Each section of the book is dedicated to a specific aspect of visiting Riyadh, ranging from essential information and trip-planning tools to detailed ideas and cultural insights. Whether you're looking for practical information about getting around the city, the best places to eat and shop, or interesting cultural events, you'll find it all right here.

Throughout the book, you will find handy maps, practical advice, and language primers to help you understand and appreciate Riyadh. So, whether you're going on a single trip, a family holiday, or a romantic getaway, let this book be your trusted friend as you discover the delights of Riyadh and create memories that will last a lifetime.

In the following sections, we'll go deeper into the various aspects of traveling in Riyadh, providing you with critical insights, suggestions, and resources to ensure a memorable vacation. So sit back, unwind, and let the Riyadh Travel Guide be your ticket to adventure in this wonderful city.

ESSENTIAL INFORMATION

Location and Geography

Riyadh, Saudi Arabia's capital city, is located in the heart of the Arabian Peninsula. Riyadh, located on the Najd Plateau, is surrounded by vast expanses of desert area known for its high temperatures and difficult terrain. The city's strategic location has long made it a significant hub for trade, economics, and cultural contact on the Arabian Peninsula.

Riyadh's scenery is characterized by its vast urban sprawl, which is punctuated by tall buildings, modern infrastructure, and bustling commercial districts. However, parts of Riyadh's rich history and cultural legacy can still be found in the metropolitan area, ranging from old defenses and mud-brick settlements to beautiful oases and date palm farms.

Riyadh's central location also makes it an excellent base for seeing other parts of Saudi Arabia, such as the stunning valleys of Asir, the ancient towns of Jeddah and Mecca, and the pristine beaches of the Red Sea coast.

Climate & Weather

Riyadh lives in a harsh desert climate with scorching temperatures and little rain all year. Summers in Riyadh are frequently long, dry, and extremely hot, with temperatures rising well above 40 degrees Celsius (104 degrees Fahrenheit) during the day. At the height of summer, temperatures can easily approach 50 degrees Celsius (122 degrees Fahrenheit).

Winters in Riyadh are mild and brief, with daytime temperatures ranging from 20 to 25 degrees Celsius (68 to 77 degrees Fahrenheit). However, nights can be cool, especially during the winter months of December and January, with temperatures dropping to around 10-15 degrees Celsius (50-59 Fahrenheit).

Given its dry climate, Riyadh receives very little rainfall, with the majority of it falling during the winter months. Visitors should be prepared for extreme heat and dry conditions, especially if traveling during the summer, and should take precautions to stay hydrated and protect themselves from the sun.

Getting In and Around Riyadh

Riyadh is served by King Khalid International Airport (RUH), which is approximately 35 kilometers (22 miles) north of the city center. As Saudi Arabia's largest airport, King Khalid International Airport provides both domestic and international flights, connecting Riyadh to destinations throughout the world.

Guests can easily travel from the airport to the city center via taxi, private shuttle, or rental car. Furthermore, Riyadh is well-connected to other major cities in Saudi Arabia by a network of roads and trains, making it easy to travel between locations within the kingdom.

In Riyadh, public transportation options include buses, taxis, and ride-hailing services such as Uber and Careem. However, the most convenient and efficient way to get around the city is to rent a car or hire a private driver. Riyadh's extensive road network and well-maintained roadways make commuting relatively uncomplicated; nonetheless, traffic congestion may be an issue during peak hours.

Visa requirements

Travelers planning to visit Riyadh must get a visa before arriving unless they are citizens of one of the countries eligible for visa-free entry or electronic visas. Visa requirements change depending on the traveler's nationality, purpose of visit, and length of stay, so check the latest visa limitations and criteria before planning your trip.

Most people obtain a tourist visa to Saudi Arabia by applying through the country's online visa website or an embassy or consulate in their own country. Tourist visas are often valid for several entries and allow tourists to stay in the kingdom for up to 90 days, with the option of extending their stay if necessary.

Currency and Money Matters

Saudi Arabia's currency is the Saudi riyal (SAR), also abbreviated as "SR" or "ريال". Each riyal is divided into 100 halalas. Banknotes are available in denominations of 1, 5, 10, 50, 100, and 500 riyals, while coins come in denominations of 5, 10, 25, and 50 halala.

ATMs are widely available across Riyadh, particularly in retail malls, hotels, and commercial districts, and they accept major credit and debit cards. Currency exchange services are also available via banks, exchange bureaus, and hotels, though fees may differ depending on the provider.

Credit and debit cards are widely accepted in Riyadh, particularly at hotels, restaurants, and large retailers. However, it is always a good idea to keep some cash on hand for little purchases and transactions, especially when visiting local markets and smaller establishments.

Communication

The official language of Saudi Arabia is Arabic, but English is widely spoken and understood, particularly in metropolitan areas such as Riyadh. Signs, restaurants, and other important information are typically offered in both Arabic and English, making it relatively easy for English-speaking tourists to navigate the city.

Mobile and internet connection is reliable and widely available across Riyadh, with many local telecom operators offering prepaid SIM cards and mobile data plans to travelers. Wi-Fi is also available in most hotels, restaurants, cafés, and public areas, allowing travelers to stay connected during their stay in Riyad.

Safety Tips

Riyadh is often regarded as a safe and secure city for tourists, with low crime rates and a strong emphasis on security and law enforcement. However, like with any large city, it is vital to exercise caution and common sense to ensure a safe and enjoyable visit.

Here are some basic safety advice for visitors to Riyadh:

Respect local customs and traditions, especially regarding dress code, public behavior, and connections with locals.

Be aware of cultural sensitivity, particularly during religious holidays and festivals.

Stay informed about current events and developments, especially in areas affected by political unrest or security concerns.

Avoid public rallies, marches, and gatherings, as these might pose substantial safety risks for tourists.

Keep valuables and personal belongings safe, especially in congested or tourist areas, to reduce the risk of theft or pickpocketing.

Follow traffic laws and regulations while driving or crossing the street, and use caution when taking public transportation or walking in congested areas.

Following these simple safety rules and remaining vigilant throughout your stay in Riyadh can help you have a secure, happy, and worry-free holiday in Saudi Arabia's capital city.

ULTIMATE EXPERIENCES GUIDE IN RIYADH

Riyadh's top attractions

Riyadh, Saudi Arabia's bustling capital city, has a wide range of activities to suit visitors of all interests and preferences. Riyadh offers a variety of activities that showcase the city's rich past, vibrant culture, and dynamic energy.

Diriyah

Diriyah, located on the outskirts of Riyadh, is a UNESCO World Heritage Site and one of the city's most well-known attractions. This historic area is famous for its mud-brick structures, narrow lanes, and medieval defenses, which provide tourists with a glimpse into Saudi Arabia's rich history and legacy. Highlights in Diriyah include the At-Turaif District, the Al-Bujairi Quarter, and the Imam Muhammad bin Abdul Wahhab Mosque.

Kingdom Center Tower
Standing tall among Riyadh's skyline, the Kingdom Centre Tower is a modern architectural marvel and a symbol of the city's rapid progress. Visitors can take an elevator to the observation deck on the 99th floor, where they can enjoy panoramic views of the city below. The Kingdom Centre Tower also has premium shopping malls, restaurants, and entertainment options, making it a popular destination for both locals and visitors.

Al-Masmak Fortress
The Al-Masmak Fortress, located in Riyadh's city center, is a historic relic from the nineteenth century. This beautiful bastion played a critical role in Saudi Arabia's unification and serves as a symbol of the city's perseverance and strength. Visitors can explore the fortress's well-preserved architecture, exhibitions, and relics, which provide insights into Riyadh's rich history and cultural legacy.

National Museum
The National Museum of Saudi Arabia is a must-see destination for history buffs and culture aficionados. This cutting-edge museum

displays Saudi Arabia's extensive past, ranging from ancient treasures to contemporary exhibits. The Kingdoms Gallery, the Hall of Manuscripts, and the Islamic Art Gallery are among the museum's highlights, featuring artifacts, manuscripts, and artworks from the country's rich cultural history.

Riyadh Galleria Mall

Riyadh Gallery Mall is the city's most popular shopping destination. This enormous mall offers a diverse selection of global and local brands, chic boutiques, and specialist shops, making it a shopper's paradise. In addition to shopping, tourists may enjoy dining at high-end restaurants, watching the latest blockbuster films at the cinema, or engaging in recreational activities such as arcades and bowling alleys.

Edge of the World

Nature lovers and adventurers would not want to miss the opportunity to see the Edge of the World, a breathtaking geological feature located just outside Riyadh. This spectacular natural marvel features towering cliffs, rocky terrain, and panoramic views that stretch as far as the eye can see. Visitors can walk, rock climb, or simply enjoy the breathtaking scenery, making it a popular destination for both outdoor lovers and photographers.

Riyadh Zoo
Riyadh Zoo is ideal for families and animal aficionados, with a diverse collection of species from around the world. Visitors can explore themed exhibits such as the African Savannah, Asian Rainforest, and Arabian Desert, where they can see a variety of animals including lions, tigers, elephants, and more. The zoo also offers educational programs, guided tours, and interactive activities to visitors of all ages.

Al-Bujairi Quarter
Al Bujairi Quarter is a historic quarter located in the heart of Riyadh, on the banks of the Wadi Hanifah. This attractive district is home to old mud-brick houses, twisting alleys, and bustling souks, giving visitors a glimpse into Riyadh's cultural history. Al Bujairi Quarter's highlights include the Al Bujairi Souq, where visitors may shop for traditional handicrafts, textiles, and souvenirs, as well as modest cafés and restaurants serving authentic Saudi cuisine.

Al-Hokair Land

Al Hokair Land is the ideal destination for family-friendly fun and entertainment in Riyadh. This big amusement park offers a wide range of rides, attractions, and activities for visitors of all ages, such as roller coasters, water slides, arcades, and more. In addition to thrill coasters, Al Hokair Land hosts live music, shows, and events all year, making it a popular destination for families, groups, and thrill seekers alike.

Al-thumairi Gate

Al-Thumairi Gate, one of the few preserved gates of the ancient city wall, has significant historical and cultural value in Riyadh. This historic entrance serves as a tangible link to the city's history, giving visitors a glimpse into Riyadh's rich cultural and architectural heritage. Surrounded by historic mud-brick residences and bustling markets, Al-Thumairi Gate provides an ideal backdrop for exploring Riyadh's vibrant cultural scene and discovering hidden gems off the beaten path.

MULTIPLE ITINERARIES

One Day in Riyadh: A Brief Overview

A one-day itinerary in Riyadh gives visitors a fast tour of the city's significant attractions and cultural features.

Begin your day by visiting the National Museum of Saudi Arabia, where you can see displays about the country's rich history and cultural legacy.

Next, visit the Al-Masmak Fortress, a historic location that played an important role in Saudi Arabia's unification.

Take a leisurely stroll around Al Bujairi Quarter, a picturesque region on the banks of the Wadi Hanifah, and explore the historic souks and cafés.

Visit the Kingdom Centre Tower and take an elevator to the observation deck for panoramic views of the city skyline.

Finish your day with supper at a local restaurant, where you can eat authentic Saudi food while taking in the vibrant atmosphere of Riyadh's eating scene.

Two to Three-Day Itinerary

With two to three days in Riyadh, visitors can explore the city's cultural attractions and outdoor activities.

Day 1:

- Start your day with a tour of Diriyah, a UNESCO World Heritage Site known for its unique mud-brick buildings and historical defenses.
- Explore the At-Turaif District and Al-Bujairi Quarter before heading to the Imam Muhammad bin Abdul Wahhab Mosque.
- Spend the day at the National Museum of Saudi Arabia, where you can learn about the country's history and culture through interactive exhibits and relics.

Day 2:
Begin your day with a visit to the Edge of the World, a remarkable natural formation just outside Riyadh that offers trekking and panoramic views of the surrounding area.

Return to the city and visit the Riyadh Gallery Mall for shopping, dining, and entertainment.

Finish your day with a visit to the Al Hokair Land amusement park, which offers rides, attractions, and family-friendly entertainment.

Five Days or More of In-Depth Exploration

Tourists who spend five days or longer in Riyadh can immerse themselves in the city's myriad attractions and activities, as well as visit nearby places and take day trips.

Day 1-3:
- Follow the two to three-day itinerary outlined above, focusing on Riyadh's key attractions, cultural sites, and outdoor excursions.

Day 4:

- Take a day trip to the historic city of Al-Diriyah, located just outside of Riyadh, and see its old palaces, museums, and cultural institutions.

Visit the Murabba Palace, King Abdulaziz's former palace, to learn about Saudi royal history.

Day 5:
- Spend your final day in Riyadh exploring the city's contemporary attractions, including the King Fahd Cultural Centre, the Riyadh Zoo, and the King Abdulaziz Historical Centre.

- End your tour with a leisurely walk down Riyadh Boulevard, where you may shop, eat, and watch entertainment before leaving the city.

Family Friendly Itinerary

Riyadh has a plethora of family-friendly attractions and activities that appeal to visitors of all ages.

Begin your day with a visit to the Riyadh Zoo, where you may see a wide variety of animals from throughout the world.

Next, head to Al Hokair Land, a massive amusement park with rides, activities, and entertainment for the whole family.

Enjoy a picnic lunch at King Abdullah Park, a beautiful green space with playgrounds, walking pathways, and recreational facilities.

In the afternoon, visit the National Museum of Saudi Arabia to learn about the country's history and culture through interactive exhibits and displays.

Finish the day with supper at a family-friendly restaurant, where you can sample traditional

Saudi cuisine and unwind after a day of sightseeing.

Solo Traveler's Guide

Solo tourists to Riyadh may enjoy exploring the city at their leisure, immersed in its rich history, culture, and culinary delights.

Begin your day by touring the old Al-Masmak Fortress and learning about its significance in Saudi Arabian history.

Spend the morning exploring the vibrant souks and marketplaces of Al Bujairi Quarter, where you can purchase traditional handicrafts, fabrics, and souvenirs.

Enjoy lunch at a local restaurant, where you may sample authentic Saudi cuisine and mingle with locals.

In the afternoon, visit the Kingdom Centre Tower and enjoy panoramic views of the cityscape from the observation deck.

Finish your day with a leisurely stroll down Riyadh Boulevard, where you may shop, eat, and watch entertainment before retiring to your accommodations for the evening.

HONEST RECOMMENDATIONS FROM LOCALS

Best Restaurants and Cafes

Residents recommend visiting Najd Village for a true sample of traditional Saudi cuisine. This restaurant offers a cozy atmosphere and classic dishes including Mandi, Kabsa, and Samboosa. The rustic atmosphere and attentive service make it popular with both locals and tourists.

Tahlia Street, known as Riyadh's culinary hub, is home to a diverse range of restaurants and cafés catering to all tastes and budgets. Tahlia Street provides something for everyone, from high-end restaurants to casual cafes and street food vendors. Locals recommend exploring the street's vibrant culinary scene and sampling a variety of cuisines.

Shay Al Shaya is a popular choice among Saudis for a traditional breakfast. This well-known café serves freshly brewed Arabic coffee and a variety of classic breakfast foods such as Ful Medames, Balaleet, and Hares. The lovely atmosphere and great service make it a popular choice for starting the day off right.

Al Nakheel Mall: Located in the heart of Riyadh, Al Nakheel Mall offers a diverse range of dining options, including fast food franchises and high-end restaurants. Locals recommend visiting the mall's food court, which offers a variety of foreign cuisines as well as local favorites such as Shawarma, Falafel, and Grilled Kebab.

Bait Al Faris: For a taste of genuine Saudi friendliness, locals recommend Bait Al Faris. This family-owned restaurant focuses on serving authentic Arabian cuisine in a comfortable setting. Bait Al Faris offers a gastronomic journey through Saudi Arabia's rich culinary legacy, from delightful appetizers to savory main meals and delectable desserts.

Top Hotels and Accommodations

The Ritz-Carlton Riyadh is a premium hotel located in the heart of the city, known for its spectacular suites, exceptional service, and world-class amenities. With spacious apartments, great dining venues, a luxury spa, and a stunning outdoor pool, the Ritz-Carlton Riyadh offers a truly sumptuous experience for discerning tourists.

Al Faisaliah Hotel: Located in the upmarket Olaya neighborhood, the Al Faisaliah Hotel is a landmark hotel known for its distinctive glass sphere design and luxurious suites. The hotel offers spacious rooms and suites, gourmet dining options, and a range of recreational amenities such as a rooftop pool, fitness center, and spa.

Four Seasons Hotel Riyadh: Nestled in lovely gardens in the premium Kingdom Centre Tower, the Four Seasons Hotel Riyadh offers a tranquil refuge in the heart of the city. The hotel's magnificent rooms and suites include modern amenities and stunning views of the city skyline. Guests can enjoy outstanding eating establishments, a premium spa, and personalized service that meets every demand.

Marriott Riyadh Diplomatic Sector: Located in Riyadh's diplomatic district, the Marriott Riyadh Diplomatic Quarter is a modern hotel that offers pleasant rooms and easy access to the city's economic and cultural attractions. The hotel offers spacious accommodations, a variety of dining options, and extensive meeting and event space, making it ideal for both business and leisure travelers.

Centro Olaya by Rotana is recommended by locals for guests looking for low-cost accommodations without losing quality. This stylish budget hotel offers modern accommodations, a variety of dining options, and convenient amenities such as a workout facility, business center, and complimentary Wi-Fi. Centro Olaya, located in the renowned Olaya sector, provides easy access to Riyadh's shopping, dining, and entertainment options.

Vibrant nightlife spots

Tahlia Street is the hub of Riyadh's nightlife, with a thriving array of clubs, cafés, and entertainment establishments. Tahlia Street has something for everyone, whether you want to listen to live music, dance at clubs, or relax in calm lounges. Locals recommend visiting the street's diverse mix of establishments and spending the night out with friends.

Al Khobar Corniche, located along the picturesque waterfront, is a favorite spot for nightly strolls and outdoor dining. The promenade is lined with cafés, restaurants, and shisha lounges, where inhabitants gather to enjoy the fresh sea air and spectacular views of the Arabian Gulf. Visitors can enjoy delicious seafood meals, drink refreshing beverages, and soak up the lively atmosphere of the Corniche.

King Abdullah Park is a large recreational space that comes to life at night with a variety of activities and events. The park features beautifully planned gardens, walking routes, and open-air amphitheaters where visitors may see live performances, concerts, and cultural activities. Locals recommend going to the park in the evening to appreciate its vibrant energy and joyous environment.

Al Faisaliah Tower: The iconic Al Faisaliah Tower is home to a variety of upscale dining and entertainment businesses with spectacular views of the city skyline. Visitors can eat delicious food in the tower's rotating restaurant, drink cocktails at the rooftop bar, or dance the night away at one of the tower's upscale nightclubs. With its magnificent setting and breathtaking views, Al Faisaliah Tower is a popular destination for rich entertainment in Riyadh.

Riyadh Boulevard: Riyadh Boulevard is a prominent nightlife destination with a diverse assortment of food, entertainment, and leisure options. The boulevard features open-air cafés, restaurants, and shops, as well as outdoor performance locations where tourists may enjoy live music, cultural activities, and street performances. Locals recommend visiting Riyadh Boulevard in the evening to enjoy the lively atmosphere and socialize with friends and family.

Shopping Destinations

Kingdom Centre Mall is one of Riyadh's most popular shopping locations, offering a wide range of international and premium brands, as well as food, entertainment, and leisure options. The mall boasts a stunning glass facade, expansive atriums, and a variety of premium shops and department stores. Visitors can shop for clothes, gadgets, home furnishings, and more, as well as dine at gourmet restaurants and cafés.

Al Nakheel Mall: Al Nakheel Mall is a well-known shopping center in the heart of Riyadh, offering a diverse range of retail establishments, culinary options, and entertainment facilities. The mall has a contemporary design, vast interiors, and a diverse selection of retailers, including fashion boutiques, technology stores, and specialty shops. Visitors may also enjoy dining at the mall's food court, watching movies at the cinema, or playing arcade games.

Riyadh Gallery Mall: Riyadh Gallery Mall is another must-see destination for shoppers, with a diverse selection of retail establishments, dining options, and entertainment facilities. The mall boasts a modern design, spacious interiors, and a diverse choice of shops to suit every taste and budget. Visitors can shop for clothing, accessories, gadgets, and more, as well as dine at the mall's restaurants and cafés.

Al Tahlia Street is known as Riyadh's best shopping district, with a diverse selection of boutiques, shops, and specialty businesses. The Boulevard is lined with high-end fashion stores, designer labels, and luxury brands, as well as local artisans and craftsmen selling traditional handicrafts and souvenirs. Visitors can walk down the street, browse the shops, and buy unique treasures to take home.

Hayat Mall: Hayat Mall is a well-known shopping center in Riyadh's western district, offering a diverse range of retail establishments, culinary options, and entertainment facilities. The mall has a contemporary design, spacious interiors, and a diverse choice of businesses to suit every taste and budget. Visitors can shop for clothing, accessories, gadgets, and more, as well as dine at the mall's restaurants and cafés.

Performing Arts Venues

King Fahd Cultural Centre: The King Fahd Cultural Centre is Riyadh's premier performing arts venue, hosting a variety of concerts, theater plays, and cultural events all year. The center is equipped with cutting-edge facilities such as a music hall, theater, and exposition rooms, as well as outdoor performance grounds and gardens. Visitors can enjoy performances by local and international artists, as well as cultural festivals and events celebrating Saudi Arabia's rich history and diversity.

Riyadh Opera House: The Riyadh Opera House is a cutting-edge performing arts complex located in the middle of the city, offering a diverse range of opera, ballet, classical music, and dramatic performances. The opera house boasts a contemporary design, world-class acoustics, and cutting-edge technology capabilities, making it a popular destination for performing arts enthusiasts. Visitors can enjoy concerts by well-known artists and groups from around the world, as well as educational programs and workshops for aspiring artists.

The Princess Nora bint Abdul Rahman University Theatre is a contemporary performing arts facility located on Princess Nora bint Abdul Rahman University's campus. The theater hosts a variety of shows, including plays, musicals, dance recitals, and concerts with local and international performers. The Princess Nora bint Abdul Rahman University Theatre, with its cutting-edge facilities and diverse programming, is a vibrant hub for cultural exchange and creative expression in Riyadh.

The Al-Yamamah University Auditorium is a multifunctional performing arts facility located on the campus of Al-Yamamah University. The auditorium hosts a wide range of events and performances, such as concerts, seminars, conferences, and theatrical productions. The Al-Yamamah University Auditorium, with its modern amenities and variable seating configurations, provides a vibrant space for creative and intellectual engagement, contributing to Riyadh's cultural landscape.

The Prince Sultan University Theatre is a contemporary performing arts facility located on the Prince Sultan University campus. The theater hosts a variety of shows, including plays, musicals, dance recitals, and concerts with local and international performers. With cutting-edge facilities and comprehensive programming, Prince Sultan University Theatre is a thriving hub for creative expression and cultural interaction in Riyadh.

Recreational activities.

Wadi Hanifah is a beautiful valley on the outskirts of Riyadh that offers a wide range of outdoor recreational activities for people to enjoy. The valley includes lush vegetation, flowing streams, and picturesque picnic sites, making it ideal for hiking, picnics, and bird watching. Visitors can also explore the valley's network of hiking trails, cycling paths, and natural attractions like waterfalls, rock formations, and animal habitats.

Riyadh's Parks and Gardens: Riyadh has a number of parks and gardens that offer residents and visitors alike a peaceful reprieve from the hustle and bustle of daily life. Popular parks include King Abdullah Park, Al-Malaz Park, and Al-Salam Park, which all have large green areas, playgrounds, and recreational facilities. Picnics, running, cycling, and leisurely strolls can all be enjoyed among the beautifully manicured gardens, blossoming trees, and picturesque panoramas.

Riyadh's Golf Courses: Riyadh has a number of world-class golf courses where golfers can tee off amid breathtaking desert scenery and lush green fairways. Riyadh Golf Courses and Dirab Golf & Country Club are popular golf courses with challenging layouts, excellent amenities, and breathtaking views of the surrounding countryside. Visitors can play golf, learn from expert instructors, or relax in the clubhouses and restaurants that overlook the courses.

Riyadh's Sports Clubs: Riyadh has a variety of sports clubs and recreational facilities, giving both locals and tourists the opportunity to stay active and healthy all year. The Riyadh Equestrian Club, Riyadh Tennis Club, and Riyadh Shooting Club are popular sports clubs that offer a variety of activities and programs to members of all ages and skill levels. Visitors can enjoy horseback riding, tennis, shooting, swimming, and other sports and leisure activities with cutting-edge facilities and expert coaching.

Riyadh's Fitness Centers and Gyms: Riyadh has a wide range of fitness centers and gyms, giving both locals and tourists the opportunity to stay active and healthy. Popular fitness facilities include Fitness First, Gold's Gym, and Fitness Time, which provide a range of workout courses, exercise equipment, and personal training services. Visitors can enjoy cardio, strength training, yoga, pilates, and other fitness activities in a welcoming and stimulating environment.

Side Trips and Day Excursions

Al-Diriyah, a UNESCO World Heritage Site just outside of Riyadh, is one of the city's most well-known attractions. Visitors can explore the historic district's mudbrick houses, historical fortifications, and cultural attractions, such as the At-Turaif District, Al-Bujairi Quarter, and Imam Muhammad bin Abdul Wahhab Mosque.

The Edge of the World is a stunning natural formation located just outside of Riyadh that offers tourists the opportunity to explore high cliffs, rocky terrain, and panoramic views. Adventurers can go trekking, rock climbing, or simply enjoy the breathtaking scenery of the desert region.

Red Sand Dunes: The Red Sand Dunes are a popular destination for outdoor enthusiasts and adventurers, offering visitors the opportunity to see rolling dunes, dramatic landscapes, and desert wilderness. Sandboarding, dune bashing, camel riding, and other leisure activities are available for visitors to enjoy in the stunning desert environment.

The Al Qassim area is a stunning location northeast of Riyadh, known for its lush oasis, abundant agriculture, and traditional villages. Visitors can discover the region's agricultural history, tour date farms and orchards, and sample local specialties such as fresh dates, honey, and traditional sweets.

Ancient Villages: Riyadh is surrounded by ancient villages and towns, giving visitors the opportunity to see traditional architecture, historical sites, and cultural icons. Al-Majmaah, Ushaiger, and Al Ghat are popular villages with historic mud-brick houses, meandering alleys, and cultural attractions that reflect Saudi Arabia's rich history and traditions.

WHAT TO EAT AND DRINK

Traditional Saudi cuisine

Saudi cuisine is deeply rooted in the country's rich cultural heritage and Bedouin traditions, with a diverse range of flavors, ingredients, and culinary styles. Traditional Saudi dishes are known for their powerful spices, fragrant herbs, and rich flavors, which reflect the country's nomadic culture and desert environment.

Mandi is a traditional Saudi dish made of tender, slow-cooked meat (typically lamb or chicken) served over aromatic basmati rice. The meat is marinated in a blend of spices, including cardamom, cloves, cinnamon, and bay leaves, and then cooked in a tandoor oven or traditional clay pot until soft and fragrant. Mandi is occasionally garnished with toasted almonds, caramelized onions, and fresh herbs and served with a side of tangy tomato sauce or spicy chili paste.

Kabsa is another well-known Saudi dish that reflects the country's rich culinary history. This flavorful rice dish is made with long-grain rice, delicate meat (usually chicken, lamb, or goat), and a fragrant blend of spices such as cumin, coriander, turmeric, and black pepper. Kabsa is often served with a side of tangy tomato sauce, mixed vegetables, and toasted almonds, resulting in a filling and aromatic dinner enjoyed by both residents and visitors.

Khubz, also known as Arabic flatbread, is a staple of Saudi cuisine and is frequently served as a versatile complement to main dishes. This soft, fluffy bread is made using wheat flour, water, yeast, and salt, then baked in a hot oven until golden brown and somewhat crispy on the outside. Khubz pairs well with savory stews, grilled meats, and traditional dips like hummus, baba ghanoush, and labneh, making it an essential part of any Saudi dinner.

Harees is a warm porridge-like meal that is popular during Ramadan and other special occasions in Saudi Arabia. Harees is a simple blend of wheat, meat (usually chicken or lamb), and spices that is slow-cooked until creamy and smooth, resulting in a substantial and wholesome meal that is enjoyed by both young and old. Harees is typically served with a drizzle of ghee or clarified butter and a sprinkle of cinnamon or nutmeg, which adds richness and flavor to this traditional Saudi dish.

Sambousek: Sambousek is a savory pastry popular throughout the Middle East, particularly Saudi Arabia. These triangular-shaped pastries are frequently filled with a variety of ingredients, including minced beef, cheese, spinach, or potatoes, and deep-fried till golden brown and crispy. Sambousek is typically served as an appetizer or snack, with a side of tahini sauce or hot chili dip, making it a delicious and satisfying treat for any occasion.

Popular Local Dishes

Shawarma is a popular Saudi street food meal consisting of thinly sliced meat (typically lamb, chicken, or beef) marinated in spices and slow-roasted on a vertical spit. The meat is frequently served in a warm pita or flatbread, with a variety of accompaniments including fresh veggies, pickles, and tahini sauce. Shawarma is popular among both residents and tourists due to its rich flavors and pleasant textures.

Falafel: Another popular street snack in Saudi Arabia, falafel is made from mashed chickpeas or fava beans that are seasoned with herbs, spices, and aromatics before being formed into tiny balls and deep-fried until crispy and golden brown. Falafel is frequently served in a warm pita or flatbread with a variety of toppings including lettuce, tomatoes, cucumbers, and tahini sauce. This vegetarian meal is a popular choice for lunch or a quick snack on the go.

Kushari: Kushari is a substantial and satisfying meal popular in Saudi Arabia and other Middle Eastern and North African nations. This delicious dinner consists of rice, lentils, pasta, and chickpeas served with a spicy tomato sauce, caramelized onions, and fried onions. Kushari is typically served with a side of pickled vegetables and a drizzle of garlic sauce or tahini, making for a lovely and soothing dinner enjoyed by people of all ages.

Mutabbaq: Mutabbaq is a savory filled pancake popular in Saudi Arabia, especially during Ramadan and other festive occasions. This delicious delicacy consists of a thin, crispy pancake filled with a tasty combination of minced beef, onions, and spices, which is then folded over and fried till golden brown and crispy. Mutabbaq is typically served with a side of tangy tomato sauce or spicy chili dip, making it a delicious and satisfying lunch at any time of day.

Hummus is a popular dip and spread in Saudi Arabia, made from cooked chickpeas blended with tahini (sesame paste), olive oil, lemon juice, garlic, and seasonings until smooth and creamy. Hummus is frequently served as an appetizer or snack, usually with warm pita bread, fresh vegetables, or falafel. Because of its creamy texture and powerful spices, this healthy and tasty dinner is popular with both locals and visitors.

Street Food Delights

Falafel is a popular street food delicacy in Saudi Arabia made from mashed chickpeas or fava beans that are seasoned with herbs, spices, and aromatics before being formed into tiny balls and deep-fried till crispy and golden brown. Falafel is frequently served in a warm pita or flatbread with a variety of toppings including lettuce, tomatoes, cucumbers, and tahini sauce. This vegetarian meal is a popular choice for lunch or a quick snack on the go.

Shawarma is another well-known street food dish in Saudi Arabia, made with thinly sliced meat (usually lamb, chicken, or beef) marinated in a variety of spices and slow-roasted on a vertical spit. The meat is frequently served in a warm pita or flatbread, with a variety of accompaniments including fresh veggies, pickles, and tahini sauce. Shawarma is popular among both residents and tourists due to its rich flavors and pleasant textures.

Kebabs are a popular street meal in Saudi Arabia, consisting of skewers of grilled meat (usually lamb, chicken, or cow) seasoned with herbs, spices, and marinades. Kebabs are sometimes served with rice, salad, grilled veggies, and a variety of sauces and condiments. Kebabs, whether eaten as a quick snack or a full meal, are a delectable and convenient option for street food enthusiasts.

Samosas are savory pastries popular in Saudi Arabia and other Middle Eastern and South Asian nations. These triangular-shaped pastries are typically filled with seasoned potatoes, peas, and, on occasion, meat before being deep-fried till crispy and golden brown. Samosas are often served as a snack or appetizer, with a variety of chutneys, sauces, and dips. Samosas are a delightful and gratifying street food pleasure that may be enjoyed alone or as part of a larger meal.

Grilled corn is a simple but delectable street meal that is popular in Saudi Arabia, especially during the summer months. Fresh ears of corn are grilled over an open flame until soft and slightly charred, then brushed with butter and sprinkled with salt, chili powder, and other spices. Grilled corn is frequently served on a stick or in a paper cone, making it a convenient and tasty snack for those on the go. Grilled corn is a pleasant and substantial street food treat that may be enjoyed as a quick snack or as a side dish.

Beverage recommendations

Arabic coffee, also known as Qahwa, is a traditional beverage in Saudi Arabia that is popular with both locals and visitors. This powerful, fragrant coffee is made with lightly roasted coffee beans and flavored with cardamom, saffron, and other spices. Arabic coffee is frequently served in little cups known as finjans, along with dates or pastries as a sign of welcome. Arabic coffee, whether drank in a primitive Bedouin tent or a modern café, is an integral part of Saudi culture and hospitality.

Saudia: A popular non-alcoholic beverage in Saudi Arabia, made from a blend of fresh fruit juices, herbs, and spices. This refreshing drink is commonly served cold or over ice and comes in a number of flavors, including lemon-mint, strawberry-basil, and mango-ginger. Saudia is a popular choice for cooling off on hot days and enjoyed by individuals of all ages.

Tamarind Juice: Tamarind juice is a tart and refreshing beverage popular in Saudi Arabia, especially in the summer. This sweet and sour drink, made from the pulp of mature tamarind fruit, is typically served chilled and mixed with sugar or honey. Tamarind juice is known for its thirst-quenching properties and is popular among both residents and tourists as a refreshing alternative to sugary sodas and soft drinks.

Laban is a traditional fermented milk beverage popular in Saudi Arabia and other parts of the Middle East. This tangy and pleasant beverage is made from yogurt that has been diluted with water and salt before fermenting to give it a slightly sour flavor. Laban is typically served cold or over ice, and it can be flavored with herbs, spices, or fruit syrups for added sweetness and complexity. Laban, whether consumed on its own or as a side dish to spicy meals, is a popular choice for cooling down and quenching thirst in the scorching desert environment.

Jallab is a sweet and fruity beverage popular in Saudi Arabia, especially during the holy month of Ramadan. This delightful drink is made from grape molasses, rose water, and date syrup, which are mixed with water and ice to create a refreshing and hydrating beverage. Jallab is commonly topped with pine nuts, raisins, and crushed ice, which add texture and flavor to this classic drink. Jallab is a treasured beverage that people of all ages in Saudi Arabia enjoy, whether it's drunk during festive events or as a cool treat on a hot day.

WHAT TO BUY

Souvenirs and Gifts

When visiting Riyadh, there are numerous interesting souvenirs and gifts to bring home as mementos of your trip. From traditional handicrafts to contemporary gems, there's something for everyone on your shopping list.

Dates are a traditional memento from Saudi Arabia, known for their high quality and variety. Dates, whether fresh or packaged, make a delicious and culturally significant gift. Look for local date markets or specialty stores to find a diverse selection of high-quality dates, such as Ajwa, Sukkari, and Khudri.

- **Oud Perfume:** Oud, also known as agarwood, is a highly valued ingredient in traditional Arabian perfumery. Oud-based fragrances are highly sought after for their rich and exotic aroma, making them ideal gifts for loved ones. Visit one of Riyadh's many perfume stores or souks to find a diverse selection of Oud fragrances, oils, and incense.

Arabic calligraphy is a beautiful and popular art form in Saudi Arabia, featuring elaborate drawings that showcase the beauty of the Arabic language. Consider purchasing a piece of calligraphy art as a unique and thoughtful gift. Look for local artists or art shops specializing in Islamic art to find exquisite items that capture the essence of Saudi culture.

- **Camel-themed Souvenirs:** Camels continue to hold a significant place in Saudi Arabian culture, representing strength, perseverance, and hospitality. Camel-themed souvenirs, such as sculptures, artwork, and fabrics, are popular gifts among tourists. Explore Riyadh's souvenir shops and marketplaces for a variety of camel-inspired souvenirs that honor this iconic desert symbol.

Traditional Saudi clothing, such as the thobe (for men) and the abaya (for women), make for distinctive and culturally significant gifts.

Consider purchasing a finely carved thobe or abaya as a unique gift or personal memento. Look for boutiques or specialty stores that offer a diverse selection of traditional clothing styles and patterns.

Traditional handicrafts

Saudi Arabia has a rich history of traditional handicrafts that reflect the country's distinct cultural influences and creative traditions. From intricate metalwork to vibrant fabrics, here are some of the most well-known traditional handicrafts to look for in Riyadh:

Al Sadu weaving is a traditional art practiced by Bedouin women in Saudi Arabia, distinguished by its intricate geometric designs and vibrant colors. Handwoven fabrics are used to make rugs, tents, pillows, and camel purses. Look for Al Sadu weaving studios or artisanal markets in Riyadh to find beautifully crafted products that reflect this ancient trade.

Silver jewelry has a long history in Saudi Arabian culture, with artisans creating stunning pieces that are both elaborate and elegant. Traditional designs frequently feature delicate filigree work, semi-precious jewels, and symbolic patterns inspired by nature and Islamic art. Visit Riyadh's jewelry souks or artisan markets to find one-of-a-kind silver jewelry that represents the country's rich cultural heritage.

Pottery and ceramics are an important part of Saudi Arabia's artistic heritage, with artisans creating a variety of functional and decorative objects using traditional techniques. Riyadh offers a wide range of pottery, from handcrafted jars to delicately painted ceramics. Visit local pottery studios or artisan markets to find finely crafted objects showcasing Saudi Arabia's creative abilities.

- **Dallah Coffee Pots:** The dallah is a traditional Arabic coffee pot that has cultural significance in Saudi Arabia, representing hospitality and charity. These elaborate metal pots are typically covered in exquisite patterns and artistic themes, making them popular collectibles and gifts. Look for dallah coffee pots in Riyadh's antique shops, souks, and specialty stores to find one-of-a-kind items that exemplify Saudi hospitality.

Woodcarving is a traditional craft performed by experienced artists in Saudi Arabia, with exquisite designs and patterns carved into various types of wood. Woodcarving is a valuable art form that represents the country's rich cultural heritage, ranging from colorful wall panels to intricate furniture and household items. Explore Riyadh's artisan markets and craft studios to find expertly carved woodwork that celebrates Saudi Arabia's craftsmanship and creative heritage.

Shopping Districts and Markets

- **Al-Qasr Mall:** Al-Qasr Mall is one of Riyadh's most popular shopping destinations, with a wide range of retail stores, restaurants, and entertainment options. The mall has a contemporary design, spacious interiors, and a diverse choice of businesses to suit every taste and budget. Visitors can shop for clothing, accessories, gadgets, and more, as well as dine at the mall's restaurants and cafés.

- **Kingdom Centre Mall:** Kingdom Centre Mall is another must-see shopping destination in Riyadh, offering a diverse selection of international and luxury brands, as well as food, entertainment, and leisure options. The mall boasts a stunning glass facade, expansive atriums, and a variety of premium shops and department stores. Visitors can shop for clothes, gadgets, home furnishings, and more, as well as dine at gourmet restaurants and cafés.

- **Riyadh Gallery Mall:** Riyadh Gallery Mall is a well-known shopping destination in the heart of Riyadh, offering a diverse range of retail establishments, food options, and entertainment facilities. The mall boasts a modern design, spacious interiors, and a diverse choice of shops to suit every taste and budget. Visitors can shop for clothing, accessories, gadgets, and more, as well as dine at the mall's restaurants and cafés.

Deira Souk is a traditional market in Riyadh that offers a dynamic and diverse shopping experience amidst bustling streets and old buildings. The souk has a wide range of stores and kiosks selling everything from clothing and accessories to spices, perfumes, and souvenirs. Visitors can explore tiny passageways adorned with colorful displays, bargain with local merchants, and find unique souvenirs that capture the spirit of Saudi culture.

- **Al-Zal Souk:** Al-Zal Souk is another popular market in Riyadh, known for its lively atmosphere and diverse selection of goods. The souk is a network of tiny passageways and covered walkways where tourists can browse kiosks selling traditional handicrafts, textiles, jewelry, and more. Al-Zal Souk is a popular destination for both locals and visitors, offering an authentic shopping experience that reflects Saudi Arabia's rich cultural heritage.

TRIP PLANNING TOOLS AND PRACTICAL TIPS

When to Go: Best Time to Visit Riyadh

Choosing the best time to visit Riyadh can significantly improve your travel experience and ensure you get the most out of your vacation. Here's an overview of the best times to visit the city:

- **Spring (March to May):** Spring is considered one of the best months to visit Riyadh because the weather is delightfully warm and pleasant. Temperatures typically range from 20°C to 30°C (68°F to 86°F), making it ideal for outdoor activities and tourism. In addition, there will be fewer people than during peak summer months, allowing you to easily explore the city's attractions.

Fall (September to November) is another great time to visit Riyadh, with pleasant temperatures and a beautiful sky. Temperatures range from 20°C to 30°C (68°F to 86°F), making it ideal for exploring the city's outdoor attractions, including parks, gardens, and historic monuments. Fall is often associated with cultural events and festivals, allowing you to immerse yourself in the local culture and customs.

- **Winter (December to February):** While winters in Riyadh are colder than other seasons, they still provide ideal weather for outdoor activities. Daytime temperatures range between 15°C and 25°C (59°F to 77°F), with colder nights. Winter is an excellent time to visit if you prefer warmer weather and want to avoid the heat of the summer months. You'll also find lower lodging prices and fewer people during this time.

- **Avoiding Summer (June to August):** Summer in Riyadh can be extremely hot, with temperatures frequently exceeding 40°C (104°F) during the midday. The scorching heat can make outdoor activities unpleasant and exhausting, so avoid visiting Riyadh during the summer months if possible. If you do come during this time, make sure to stay hydrated, seek shade, and plan your activities for early morning or late afternoon when temperatures are lower.

Overall, the best time to visit Riyadh is in the spring or autumn, when the weather is pleasant and comfortable, and there are plenty of cultural events and outdoor activities to enjoy.

Getting Around The City

Navigating Riyadh's massive metropolis may appear overwhelming at first, but with the right transportation options, getting around the city can be relatively simple and convenient. Here is some practical advice for navigating around Riyadh:

- **Taxi:** Taxis are a popular mode of transportation in Riyadh and can be found all over the city. Look for certified taxis with meters, and make sure to confirm the fare with the driver before beginning your journey. Taxis are easily accessible in hotels, shopping malls, and tourist destinations, making them a popular mode of transportation in the city.

Ride-hailing apps such as Uber and Careem are widely used in Riyadh and offer a convenient alternative to traditional taxis. Simply download the app, enter your location, and then request a ride. Ride-hailing apps are typically more cost-effective and convenient than taxis, especially during peak hours or in areas where cabs are scarce.

- **Public Transportation:** Riyadh's public transportation system includes buses and a metro system, providing affordable and efficient options for getting around the city. The Riyadh Metro, which consists of six lines, connects key areas and attractions throughout the city. Furthermore, the Riyadh Bus Network operates a vast network of bus routes that serve various parts of the city.

- **Renting a vehicle:** If you want more freedom and independence while exploring Riyadh, consider renting a car. There are several car rental companies operating in the area, offering a diverse range of vehicles to meet your needs and budget. Keep in mind that driving in Riyadh can be challenging, especially for first-time visitors, so familiarize yourself with local traffic laws and regulations.

- **Walking and cycling:** Although Riyadh is primarily a car-centric metropolis, there are some pedestrian and bicycle-friendly areas. Discover the city's parks, promenades, and pedestrian-friendly areas on foot or by bike for a relaxing and environmentally friendly way to get around.

You can easily get around Riyadh and visit its various attractions by using a combination of taxis, ride-hailing apps, public transportation, and walking.

Tips for Beating the Crowd

Riyadh is a vibrant city that attracts visitors from all over the world, especially during peak tourist seasons. To avoid the crowds and make the most of your time in the city, consider the following suggestions:

- **Plan Ahead:** Research famous sites and places in Riyadh and make a schedule in advance. Consider going to major attractions early in the morning or late in the afternoon, when crowds are lighter.

- **Visit Off-Peak Hours:** Avoid going to major attractions during peak hours, such as weekends or holidays, when crowds are at their highest. Instead, visit sights on weekdays or early in the morning for a more peaceful and enjoyable experience.

- **Explore Lesser-Known Attractions:** While Riyadh has many well-known monuments and attractions, there are also plenty of hidden gems and lesser-known locations waiting to be discovered. Explore off-the-beaten-path districts, parks, and markets to experience the city's true culture and charm away from the crowds.

- **Book Tickets in Advance:** For popular sites and events, consider purchasing tickets in advance to secure your seat and avoid long lines. Many attractions offer online booking options, allowing you to avoid the crowds and gain priority entry.

- **Take Advantage of Early Access Tours:** Some sites offer early access or guided tours, allowing you to explore the location before it is open to the general public. Consider organizing these excursions for a more personal and engaging experience without the crowds.

You can beat the crowds and make the most of your trip to Riyadh by planning ahead of time, visiting attractions during off-peak hours, discovering lesser-known places, booking tickets in advance, and taking advantage of early access tours.

Saving Time and Money

Budget Travel Tips

Traveling to Riyadh on a budget does not imply sacrificing comfort or missing out on unique experiences. With careful planning and wise choices, you can save time and money while touring the city. Here are some affordable travel options for Riyadh:

- **Accommodation:** Consider staying in Riyadh's budget hotels, guesthouses, or hostels. Look for deals and discounts on booking websites, or look into alternative hotel options like Airbnb for more affordable and flexible lodging options.

- **Transportation:** To get around Riyadh, use public buses, metros, or ride-sharing services that are reasonably priced. To save money on transportation, avoid taking taxis or private cars for short trips and instead walk or bike.

- **Eating:** In Riyadh, visit local markets, street food vendors, and low-cost cafes to save money on dining out. Look for traditional Arabian restaurants or local cafes that serve affordable and authentic food without breaking the bank. For a low-cost dining experience, consider preparing your own meals or picnicking in parks.

- **Attractions and Activities:** Take advantage of Riyadh's free or low-cost attractions and activities, such as visiting public parks, touring museums and galleries with free admission days, or attending cultural events and festivals. Look for reduced tickets or special discounts for popular attractions, and consider purchasing city passes or tour packages for even more savings.

- **Shopping:** Check prices, negotiate with sellers, and avoid tourist traps to save money on souvenirs and gifts. Explore Riyadh's local marketplaces, souks, and artisan stores for one-of-a-kind and affordable souvenirs, handicrafts, and traditional goods that reflect the city's culture and traditions.

- **Travel Off-Season:** Consider visiting Riyadh during the off-peak tourist season to take advantage of lower hotel prices, fewer people, and cheaper flights. Shoulder seasons, such as spring and autumn, provide excellent weather and fewer people, making them ideal for a budget trip to Riyadh.

By following these budget travel recommendations, you can save both time and money while visiting Riyadh, resulting in a fantastic and affordable travel experience in the heart of Saudi Arabia.

HISTORICAL AND CULTURAL INSIGHTS

Overview of Riyadh's History

Riyadh, Saudi Arabia's capital city, has a rich and legendary history dating back thousands of years. Riyadh has changed dramatically over the years, from its humble beginnings as a small desert village to its current status as a thriving city.

The first known residents of Riyadh were the Najd tribes, who arrived around 6000 BCE. The region's strategic location along old trade routes made it a hub for business and cultural interaction, attracting merchants, visitors, and residents from the surrounding areas.

Riyadh rose to prominence in the seventh century CE as an important stop on the pilgrimage route to Mecca known as the Hajj. The city's location in the heart of the Arabian Peninsula made it an ideal rest stop for pilgrims traveling to and from Mecca, prompting the establishment of marketplaces, inns, and mosques.

Riyadh's historic history began in the mid-18th century, when the Al Saud family established control over the city. The Al Sauds, led by Sheikh Mohammed bin Saud and Sheikh Mohammed bin Abdul Wahab, transformed Riyadh into the first Saudi kingdom's capital as well as an Islamic study and government center.

Under the leadership of King Abdulaziz Al Saud, also known as Ibn Saud, Riyadh experienced rapid growth and modernization in the early twentieth century. King Abdulaziz united the many tribes and areas of the Arabian Peninsula under the banner of the Kingdom of Saudi Arabia, with Riyadh serving as its political and administrative center.

Today, Riyadh is a sophisticated city that seamlessly combines its rich cultural heritage with modern comforts and infrastructure. Visitors to Riyadh can learn more about the city's fascinating history and legacy by touring its historic sites, museums, and cultural organizations.

Cultural Etiquettes and Customs

Saudi Arabian culture is deeply rooted in Islamic traditions and rituals, which influence the people's daily lives and social interactions. Understanding and adhering to Saudi cultural etiquette is essential for visitors to Riyadh to have a positive and courteous experience. Here are some important cultural norms to keep in mind:

- **Respect for Islam:** Islam is Saudi Arabia's primary religion, and its ideas and teachings influence many aspects of daily life. Visitors should respect Islamic customs and traditions by wearing modest clothing, avoiding public displays of affection, and refraining from eating or drinking in public during the month of Ramadan.

- **Gender Segregation:** Saudi Arabia strictly enforces gender segregation in public places such as restaurants, transportation, and recreation areas. Visitors should be aware of these laws and follow them properly. Furthermore, women are expected to wear modest clothing that covers their arms, legs, and heads in public.

- **Greetings and Gestures:** In Saudi Arabia, it is customary to greet someone with the traditional Islamic greeting "As-salamu alaykum" (peace be upon you), followed by the response "Wa alaykum as-salam" (and upon you be peace). Handshakes are common between members of the same gender, but physical contact between unrelated men and women is generally avoided.

Hospitality is very important in Saudi Arabian culture, and visitors are treated with warmth, generosity, and respect. Visitors may be welcomed into homes for dinners or gatherings, where they will be served traditional Arabic coffee and dates as a sign of hospitality. It is customary to accept such invitations graciously and express gratitude for the host's generosity.

- **Respect for Authority:** In Saudi Arabian culture, authority figures, particularly government officials, religious leaders, and elders, are highly respected. Visitors should be courteous and respectful when dealing with those in positions of power, and they should avoid engaging in conduct that could be considered disrespectful or objectionable.

Tourists who follow and respect Saudi cultural etiquette and traditions can form healthy connections with the local population and gain a better understanding of Riyadh's and Saudi Arabia's rich cultural heritage.

Architectural Wonders

Riyadh is home to a diverse collection of architectural masterpieces that highlight the city's rich cultural legacy, Islamic heritage, and modern development. Riyadh's architectural environment pays tribute to its vibrant past and dynamic present, with ancient fortifications and medieval palaces alongside modern skyscrapers and futuristic monuments.

Diriyah is a UNESCO World Heritage site located on the outskirts of Riyadh, known for its well-preserved mud-brick structures, traditional Najdi architecture, and historical significance as the birthplace of the first Saudi kingdom. The complex includes old palaces, mosques, and fortifications dating back to the 18th century, as well as the renowned At-Turaif neighborhood, which served as the capital of the first Saudi kingdom.

- **Masmak Fortress:** Masmak Fortress is a historic monument located in the heart of Riyadh and dates back to the nineteenth century. The stronghold played an important role in the formation of the current Kingdom of Saudi Arabia and serves as a symbol of the city's rich history and heritage. Visitors to the stronghold and museum can learn about its significance and the events that shaped Saudi Arabia's history.

The Kingdom Centre Tower is one of Riyadh's most well-known contemporary structures, rising 302 meters above the city skyline. Designed by renowned architect Norman Foster, the tower has a distinctive elliptical shape and a magnificent glass front that reflects the surrounding scenery. Visitors to the tower's observation deck can enjoy panoramic views of Riyadh while also exploring its magnificent retail complex, eateries, and entertainment facilities.

- **Al Faisaliah Tower:** Another well-known skyscraper in Riyadh is the Al Faisaliah Tower, which stands out for its unique design and architectural beauty. The tower's spectacular glass sphere, crowned with a golden pinnacle, represents Riyadh's modernity and success. Visitors can eat at the tower's rotating restaurant, shop at its premium stores, and enjoy the stunning views of the city.

The National Museum of Saudi Arabia (NMSA) is a cultural institution dedicated to preserving and presenting Saudi Arabia's history, heritage, and culture. The museum's remarkable building, inspired by traditional Arabian architectural features, houses a significant collection of relics, exhibits, and interactive displays that document the country's rich archeological, cultural, and artistic heritage.

Riyadh's architectural treasures range from ancient fortifications and medieval palaces to modern skyscrapers and cultural organizations, providing a fascinating glimpse into the city's diverse legacy and rapid growth.

Art & Museums

Riyadh has a vibrant arts and culture scene, with numerous museums, galleries, and cultural organizations showcasing the city's rich creative heritage and modern ingenuity. From ancient relics and Islamic art to contemporary masterpieces and avant-garde performances, Riyadh offers a diverse range of creative experiences for visitors to discover and enjoy.

The King Abdulaziz Center for World Culture, also known as Ithra, is a cultural landmark in Riyadh that celebrates creativity, innovation, and knowledge sharing. The center includes a cutting-edge museum, art galleries, theaters, and performance spaces that host a variety of exhibits, events, and educational programs. Visitors can explore the center's interactive exhibits, attend seminars and lectures, and watch performances by local and international artists.

The Museum of Saudi Arabian Art is dedicated to showcasing Saudi Arabia's rich artistic heritage and cultural identity. The museum, located in Riyadh's ancient Al Murabba area, houses a diverse collection of artworks, antiques, and installations that reflect the country's distinct creative heritage, such as calligraphy, painting, sculpture, and textiles. Visitors can explore the museum's permanent and temporary exhibits to learn about Saudi Arabia's cultural history and current art scene.

The King Fahd Cultural Center is a cultural complex in Riyadh that serves as a hub for arts, entertainment, and cultural activities. The center's facilities, which include theaters, exhibition halls, and outdoor performance spaces, can accommodate a wide range of events and activities, such as concerts, theatrical plays, film screenings, and art exhibits. Visitors can watch performances by local and international artists, attend cultural events and festivals, and browse the center's art galleries and exhibits.

The Al-Turath Foundation is a cultural organization in Riyadh that works to preserve and develop Saudi Arabia's cultural history and customs. The organization organizes a variety of cultural events and activities, such as traditional music and dance performances, artisan workshops, and cultural festivals, to promote the country's distinct cultural history. Visitors can participate in cultural activities and experiences organized by the foundation to learn about Saudi Arabia's rich cultural traditions and customs.

Art Galleries and Studios: Riyadh has a thriving arts scene, with an increasing number of galleries, studios, and creative spaces showcasing the work of local and international artists. Visitors can experience a wide range of modern art forms, such as painting, sculpture, photography, and mixed media, by visiting art galleries and exhibits throughout the city. In addition, many galleries and studios offer seminars, artist presentations, and cultural events that allow you to engage with the local arts community and support emerging talent.

Riyadh's arts scene is dynamic and diverse, reflecting the city's rich cultural legacy and creative energy. It includes world-class museums and cultural institutions as well as modern art galleries and studios.

Cuisine and Culinary Tradition

Saudi Arabian cuisine is a rich tapestry of flavors, fragrances, and culinary traditions that reflect the country's diverse cultural influences and regional differences. Riyadh offers a tempting variety of culinary experiences for food enthusiasts to discover and enjoy, ranging from traditional Bedouin meals to modern takes on Arabian classics.

- **Traditional Saudi meals:** Saudi Arabian cuisine is known for its hearty and flavorful meals that reflect the country's rich culinary heritage. Traditional Saudi foods frequently include rice, lamb, poultry, and spices, which are prepared using traditional techniques and recipes passed down through generations. Some traditional Saudi dishes include Kabsa (spiced rice with meat), Mandi (slow-cooked meat and rice), and Samboosa (savory pastries stuffed with meat or vegetables).

- **Arabic Mezze:** Mezze, or small appetizer dishes, are a staple of Saudi

Arabian cuisine and are frequently served as appetizers or snacks during meals. Hummus, baba ghanoush, tabbouleh, falafel, and filled grape leaves are all common ingredients in mezze meals. These delicious and colorful meals are enjoyed as part of a communal dining experience with family and friends.

- **Saudi Breakfast:** Breakfast is an important meal in Saudi Arabian culture, and it typically includes a variety of savory and sweet dishes. A traditional Saudi breakfast might include Ful medames (fava bean stew), foul mudammas (fava bean salad), Arabic bread (like Khubz or Fatir), labneh (strained yogurt), olives, and dates. Tea or Arabic coffee is often served with breakfast as a pleasant beverage.

- **Desserts and Sweets:** Saudi Arabian cuisine is well-known for its delicious desserts and sweets, which are often served as a treat at special events and festivals. Popular Saudi desserts include

Kunafa (sweet cheese pastry), Baklava (layered pastry with almonds and honey), Basbousa (semolina cake), and Qatayef (stuffed pancakes). These rich delights are enjoyed by both residents and tourists as a delicious end to a meal.

- **Arabic Coffee and Dates:** Arabic coffee (Qahwa) and dates are integral parts of Saudi hospitality and culture. Arabic coffee is made from gently roasted coffee beans and flavored with cardamom, saffron, and other spices. It is typically served in little cups called finjans. Dates, which are abundantly grown in Saudi Arabia, are served as a symbol of welcome and hospitality to guests and visitors.

- **Saudi Street Food:** Riyadh's bustling streets are brimming with exquisite street food options that cater to all tastes and preferences. Saudi street food, which includes savory snacks like Shawarma (grilled meat wraps), Falafel (fried chickpea patties), and Kebabs (grilled meat skewers), as well as sweet treats like Luqaimat (deep-fried dough balls) and Mahalabiya (rosewater pudding), provides a flavorful and affordable dining experience for foodies on the go.

- **Arabic drinks:** Saudi Arabia offers a variety of tasty drinks that are enjoyed by both residents and tourists. Traditional Arabic beverages include Arabic coffee (Qahwa), made from gently roasted coffee beans and flavored with cardamom and saffron, and Arabic tea (Shai), made from black tea leaves and flavored with mint or spices. Other popular drinks are Jallab (sweet fruit syrup drink), Tamarind juice (tangy fruit drink), and Laban (fermented milk drink).

Overall, Riyadh's culinary scene is a vibrant tapestry of flavors, aromas, and culinary traditions that reflect the country's diverse cultural heritage and culinary influences. Riyadh offers a gourmet experience that will tantalize your taste buds and leave you wanting more.

LOCAL WRITERS' RECOMMENDATIONS

Locals recommend hidden treasures

While Riyadh has several well-known attractions and monuments, the city also has a plethora of hidden gems that people treasure but which outsiders may not be aware of. From tranquil parks and ancient areas to inviting cafés and cultural organizations, these hidden gems provide a unique glimpse into Riyadh's heart and soul.

- **Wadi Hanifa:** Nestled amid the hectic metropolis of Riyadh, Wadi Hanifa is a tranquil oasis that provides a welcome respite from the city's hustle and bustle. This lovely valley is dotted with thick vegetation, winding pathways, and beautiful views, making it a great spot for a leisurely stroll or a peaceful picnic. Locals frequently visit Wadi Hanifa to unwind, reconnect with nature, and escape the stresses of city life. Visitors can explore the wadi's walking routes, go birdwatching, or simply relax and soak up the tranquil atmosphere of this hidden treasure.

- **Al-Bujairi area:** Nestled in the heart of Riyadh's old Al-Diriyah area, the Al-Bujairi District is a charming cultural enclave that transports visitors back in time to the city's fabled past. This pedestrian-friendly area is distinguished by its classic mud-brick buildings, narrow lanes, and atmospheric souks, where artisans sell handcrafted goods and local cuisine. Visitors can walk through the winding passageways, see the restored buildings, and soak up the vibrant atmosphere of this hidden gem.

- **Riyadh's Street Art culture:** While Riyadh is not known for its street art, the city has a growing urban art culture that is gaining recognition both locally and internationally. Bright murals, graffiti artworks, and street installations adorn walls, alleys, and public spaces around the city, injecting creativity and energy into the urban landscape. Locals frequent these hidden gems to discover new artworks, support local artists, and experience the city's evolving cultural identity. Visitors can take a self-guided tour of Riyadh's street art culture or join organized street art walks to discover these hidden gems and gain insight into the city's contemporary art scene.

- **Al-Masmak Palace Museum:** While not exactly hidden, the Al-Masmak Palace Museum provides an intriguing glimpse into Riyadh's history and traditions that are sometimes overlooked by visitors. This famed fortress-turned-museum, located in the heart of the city, is a symbol of Saudi Arabia's establishment as well as a testament to its people's perseverance. The museum's exhibits, antiques, and interactive displays allow visitors to learn about the palace's storied history, the founding of the Kingdom of Saudi Arabia, and the region's rich cultural legacy. Locals frequently visit Al-Masmak Palace Museum to bond with their ancestors, learn more about their beginnings, and respect the country's founding fathers.

- **Hidden Cafes and Hangouts:** Riyadh has a thriving cafe culture, with hidden gems scattered across the city. From quiet coffee shops and trendy brunch spots to sleek dessert cafés and artisanal bakeries, these hidden gems offer a welcoming atmosphere, delicious meals, and a sense of community that keeps residents coming back for more. Visitors can discover Riyadh's secret cafe scene, try new flavors and cuisines, and connect with locals over a cup of coffee or a sweet treat. Riyadh's secret cafes and hangouts have something for everyone, whether you're looking for a quick coffee, a leisurely breakfast, or a delectable dessert.

In conclusion, Riyadh's hidden gems provide insight into the city's vibrant culture, rich history, and diverse population. From peaceful natural oasis and historic districts to vibrant street art and secret cafés, these hidden gems provide guests with unique experiences and opportunities to engage with local culture and community. Tourists that venture off the beaten path and find Riyadh's hidden gems may uncover new perspectives, form meaningful relationships, and create enduring memories of their visit to the Saudi capital.

Insider tips for exploring Riyadh.

Exploring Riyadh, Saudi Arabia's capital city, can be a fascinating and rewarding experience for tourists seeking to learn about the area's rich culture, history, and customs. To make the most of your trip to Riyadh and discover its hidden gems, consider these insider tips from locals:

- **Embrace the Local Culture:** Riyadh is a city with a rich history and Islamic tradition, and understanding the local culture is essential for experiencing the city's true character. Take the time to study about Saudi customs, traditions, and etiquette, and be respectful of local standards and sensibilities. Dress modestly, greet locals with the traditional Arabic greeting "As-salamu alaykum," and prepare to immerse yourself in Riyadh's rich cultural tapestry.

- **Explore Beyond the City Center:** While Riyadh's city center is bustling with activity and attractions, some of the city's most intriguing hidden jewels lie beyond its major neighborhoods. To locate hidden gems, historic buildings, and unique local experiences, take a detour off the main route and visit areas such as Al-Diriyah, Al-Ula, or Al-Deera. From historic forts and traditional souks to busy cultural enclaves and beautiful oases, Riyadh's lesser-known regions offer a more in-depth look at the city's history, legacy, and culture.

- **Sample the Local Cuisine:** Riyadh is a foodie's paradise, with a wide range of gastronomic delights waiting to be discovered. From traditional Saudi specialties and Arabic mezze to global cuisines and street gastronomic delights, the city has enough to satisfy every taste. Don't pass up the opportunity to try local favorites like Kabsa (spiced rice with meat), Mandi (slow-cooked pork and rice), and Kunafa (sweet cheese pastry), as well as Arabic coffee and dates, which are a staple of Saudi hospitality.

- **Embrace the Desert:** Riyadh is surrounded by vast desert landscapes, providing limitless opportunities for outdoor adventure and discovery. Take a desert safari to enjoy the beauty and tranquility of the Arabian Desert, go on an exhilarating dune bashing trip, or spend the night at a desert camp. Whether you're riding camels, sandboarding down dunes, or simply admiring the breathtaking desert landscape, embracing the desert is an essential aspect of the Riyadh experience.

- **Engage with the Local Community:** One of the best ways to truly explore Riyadh is to interact with its residents. Strike up conversations with locals, seek advice, and look for unique activities that allow you to mix with Riyadh's many communities. Connecting with the locals, whether you're seeing historic souks, attending cultural events, or participating in local traditions and customs, will enhance your experience and create lasting memories of your time in Riyadh.

By following these insider tips for visiting Riyadh, you may discover hidden jewels, have authentic experiences, and gain a deeper understanding of the Saudi capital's rich culture, history, and customs. Riyadh offers a variety of activities, like strolling through old neighborhoods, eating local cuisine, and seeing the desert.

LANGUAGE PRIMER

Useful Phrases for Travelers

When traveling to Riyadh, it may be beneficial to familiarize oneself with some basic Arabic vocabulary and phrases in order to facilitate conversation and enrich the overall vacation experience. While many people in Riyadh understand English, attempting to learn Arabic may show respect for the local culture and help you manage daily interactions more efficiently. Here are some important terms and phrases for traveling to Riyadh.

Greetings and Basic Phrases:
Marhaba (مرحبا): Hello.
Good morning, Sabah al-khayr (صباح الخير).
Masa' al-khayr (الخير) - Good evening!
Shukran (شكرا): Thank you
Afwan (عفوا): You are welcome.
Na'am (نعم): Yes
La (لا) - No
Please, Min Fadlak (من فضلك).
Goodbye, Ma'a as-salama.

Basic conversation:
Kaifa halak? (كيف حالك؟): How are you?
Ana Bikhair, Shukran. What do you want? I'm fine, thank you. And you?
Min ayna? (من أين أنت؟): Where are you from?
Ana min [your country] (أنا من [your country]): I am from [your country].
What is the difference between English and Arabic? Do you speak English?

Directions & Transportation:
Wayn al-Metro? Where is the metro?
Al-yameen (اليمين) – Right
Al-yasar (اليسار) – Left
Al-amam (الأمام): Straight forward.
Al-war'a (الوراء) – Behind
Mata yamkinuni al-wusul [destination]? When will I be able to reach [destination].
Kayfa, what is your destination? (How do I go to [destination]?

Food and Dining:
Please order from the menu.
Ma, hadha? (ما هذا؟): What is this?
I am in need of [dish/ingredient].
Arju al-hummus (أرجو الحمص): I would like hummus.

94

Al-ma'a (الماء): Water
Ash-shay (الشاي): Tea
Qahwa (قهوة) – Coffee

Shopping and bargaining:
Bikam hadha? (بكم هذا؟): How much is this?
Hatha ghali aw Rahin? (Is this expensive or cheap?
Yajeb an aqra' al-sa'a (يجب أن أقرأ الساعة) - I must read the time
La, shukran (شكرا) - No, thank you.
Asif, la'astaTii' al-ana (آسف، لا أستطيع الآن) - Sorry, I can't right now.

Emergency situations:
Al-Musa'ada! (المساعدة!) - Help!
Atahtaru (أتحتاج إلى الطبيب): I need a doctor.
Al-hurub! (الحريق!) - Fire!
Al-ssira' (السرقة): Theft.
Al-khatir! (الخطر!) - Danger!

Numbers and Counting:
Wahid (واحد) – One
Ithnayn (اثنين): Two
Thalatha (ثلاثة): Three
Arba'a (أربعة) – Four
Khamsa (خمسة) – Five

Sitta (ستة) – Six.
Saba'a (سبعة) – Seven.
Thamanya (ثمانية) – Eight
Tis'a (تسعة) – Nine
Ashara (عشرة) – Ten

By learning and practicing these fundamental Arabic terms and phrases, you may improve your vacation experience in Riyadh, engage with locals, and handle everyday encounters with confidence and ease.

Essential Arabic Phrases for Daily Situations

When visiting Riyadh, having a basic command of Arabic will greatly enhance your vacation experience and allow you to easily navigate daily situations. While many individuals in Riyadh speak English, attempting to converse in Arabic demonstrates respect for the local culture and may result in more meaningful relationships with locals. Here are some important Arabic words for various scenarios that visitors to Riyadh could find useful:

Greetings and Basic Phrases:
Marhaba (مرحبا): Hello.
Good morning, Sabah al-khayr (صباح الخير).
Masa' al-khayr (الخير) - Good evening!
Ahlan wa sahlan (أهلا سهلا) - Welcome.
Shukran (شكرا): Thank you
Afwan (عفوا): You are welcome.
Please, Min Fadlak (من فضلك).
Na'am (نعم): Yes
La (لا) - No
Goodbye, Ma'a as-salama.

Basic conversation:
Kaifa halak? (كيف حالك؟): How are you?
Ana Bikhair, Shukran. What do you want? I'm fine, thank you. And you?
Min ayna? (من أين أنت؟): Where are you from?
Ana min [your country] (أنا من [your country]): I am from [your country].
What is the difference between English and Arabic? Do you speak English?

Directions & Transportation:
Wayn al-Metro? Where is the metro?
Al-yameen (اليمين) – Right
Al-yasar (اليسار) – Left
Al-amam (الأمام): Straight forward.

Al-war'a (الوراء) – Behind
Mata yamkinuni al-wusul [destination]? When will I be able to reach [destination]?
Kayfa, what is your destination? (How do I go to [destination]?

Food and Dining:
Please order from the menu.
Ma, hadha? (ما هذا؟): What is this?
I am in need of [dish/ingredient].
Arju al-hummus (أرجو الحمص): I would like hummus.
Al-ma'a (الماء): Water
Ash-shay (الشاي): Tea
Qahwa (قهوة) – Coffee

Shopping and bargaining:
Bikam hadha? (بكم هذا؟): How much is this?
Hatha ghali aw Rahin? (Is this expensive or cheap?
Yajeb an aqra' al-sa'a (يجب أن أقرأ الساعة) - I must read the time
La, shukran (شكرا) - No, thank you.
Asif, la'astaTii' al-ana (آسف، لا أستطيع الآن) - Sorry, I can't right now.
Emergency situations:

98

Al-Musa'ada! (المساعدة!) - Help!
Atahtaru (أتحتاج إلى الطبيب): I need a doctor.
Al-hurub! (الحريق!) - Fire!
Al-ssira' (السرقة): Theft.
Al-khatir! (الخطر!) - Danger!

Numbers and Counting:
Wahid (واحد) – One
Ithnayn (اثنين): Two
Thalatha (ثلاثة): Three
Arba'a (أربعة) – Four
Khamsa (خمسة) – Five
Sitta (ستة) – Six.
Saba'a (سبعة) – Seven.
Thamanya (ثمانية) – Eight
Tis'a (تسعة) – Nine
Ashara (عشرة) – Ten

By learning and using these simple Arabic terms to typical situations, you can manage daily interactions, engage with people, and enhance your travel experience in Riyadh. Whether you're exploring the city, dining at a local restaurant, or shopping in the souks, knowing a few Arabic words can help you make lasting connections and promote cultural exchange.

CONCLUSION

Final Thoughts About Visiting Riyadh

Visiting Riyadh is a wonderful trip full of cultural riches, historical wonders, and real hospitality. As you end your journey in Saudi Arabia's vibrant capital city, take a moment to reflect on the experiences and memories you've created. Riyadh has a distinct blend of classic charm and contemporary sophistication, making it a destination that appeals to people from all walks of life.

Riyadh's rich history and cultural legacy are among its most notable features. From ancient forts and palaces to bustling souks and medieval districts, the city is steeped in centuries of traditions and customs. Exploring Riyadh's historical landmarks provides a fascinating glimpse into the region's rich history as well as insight into the cultural fabric that shapes modern-day Saudi Arabia.

Furthermore, Riyadh's sophisticated skyline and dynamic urban environment reflect the city's rapid growth and success. Riyadh, Saudi Arabia's economic and cultural capital, is a melting pot of cultures, languages, and lifestyles. From world-class shopping malls and luxury hotels to cutting-edge architecture and a creative culinary scene, the city offers a wide range of modern services and activities for visitors to enjoy.

One of the benefits of visiting Riyadh is the opportunity to immerse yourself in local culture and mingle with the friendly people of Saudi Arabia. Whether you're eating traditional Saudi cuisine at a local restaurant, bargaining for items at a bustling market, or engaging in lively conversations with locals, Riyadh offers limitless opportunities for cultural exchange and lasting interactions.

As you say farewell to Riyadh, carry with you memories of the sites you've seen, the flavors you've tasted, and the friendships you've made along the way. Whether you're a history buff, a foodie, an adventurer, or simply an inquisitive tourist, Riyadh has something for everyone.

Your Riyadh adventure awaits!

Your Riyadh tour awaits you, inviting you to go on a journey of discovery and exploration in one of the Middle East's most charming cities. Whether you're planning a quick trip or a longer stay, Riyadh ensures an unforgettable travel experience filled with excitement, culture, and adventure.

As you explore the city, make an effort to immerse yourself in Riyadh's vibrant cultural scene, from visiting ancient landmarks to attending cultural festivals and events. Explore the antique charms of Diriyah, the bustling alleys of Al-Bathaa, and the modern marvels of the King Abdullah Financial District. Riyadh's various districts offer a kaleidoscope of experiences waiting to be discovered.

Indulge your taste buds with the wonderful flavors of Saudi cuisine, ranging from savory traditional dishes to inventive gourmet creations. Try aromatic Arabic coffee and tasty dates, enjoy the spices of a traditional Kabsa, and indulge in the rich tastes of a fragrant Mansaf. Riyadh's dining scene is a gourmet delight waiting to be explored.

Furthermore, don't pass up the opportunity to shop until you drop at Riyadh's vibrant marketplaces and stylish malls. From historic souks and bustling bazaars to luxury boutiques and designer shops, Riyadh has something for everyone's taste and budget. Riyadh has everything you're looking for, whether it's unusual presents, superb handicrafts, or the latest fashion trends.

When the day turns to night, explore the city's vibrant nightlife scene, which includes everything from stylish cafés and sophisticated lounges to exciting nightclubs and cultural performances. Dance the night away to the beats of Arabian music, sip cocktails under the stars, and immerse yourself in Riyadh's intoxicating energy.

As you go on your Riyadh vacation, embrace the spirit of exploration, curiosity, and discovery. Open your heart and mind to new experiences, make friends with the locals, and create memories to last a lifetime. Your Riyadh adventure awaits; are you prepared to answer the call?

Printed in Great Britain
by Amazon